EXPANDED EDITION

Grade 2

The *That Magnetic Dog* lesson is part of the Picture-Perfect STEM program K–2 written by the program authors and includes lessons from their award-winning series.

Additional information about using the Picture Perfect Science series, including key reading strategies, NGSS connections, and the BSCS 5E instructional model can be downloaded for free at:

That Magnetic Dog

Description

Learners explore the phenomenon that some things are attracted to a magnet and others are not. They discover through exploration that not all metals are magnetic and communicate their findings in a poster session. Then they learn by reading a nonfiction book that magnets attract iron and iron-containing materials. Finally, they learn how different types of magnets are used for different purposes, and they design their own magnetic solution to a problem.

Alignment with the *Next Generation Science Standards*

Performance Expectation		
2-PS1-1: Plan and conduct an investigation to describe and classify different kinds of materials by their observable properties.		
Science and Engineering Practices	**Disciplinary Core Idea**	**Crosscutting Concept**
Analyzing and Interpreting Data Compare predictions (based on prior experiences) to what occurred (observable events). **Obtaining, Evaluating, and Communicating Information** Read grade-appropriate texts and/or use media to obtain scientific and/or technical information to determine patterns in and/or evidence about the natural and designed worlds.	**PS1.A: Structure and Properties of Matter** Matter can be described and classified by its observable properties.	**Patterns** Patterns in the natural and human-designed world can be observed, used to describe phenomena, and used as evidence.

Note: The activities in this lesson will help students move toward the performance expectation listed, which is the goal after multiple activities. However, the activities will not by themselves be sufficient to reach the performance expectation.

Featured Picture Books

TITLE: ***That Magnetic Dog***
AUTHOR: **Bruce Whatley**
ILLUSTRATOR: **Bruce Whatley**
PUBLISHER: **Angus & Robertson**
YEAR: **1994**
GENRE: **Story**
SUMMARY: *Skitty is a dog with "magnetic" qualities. She doesn't attract metal, like keys and spoons. She attracts food.*

TITLE: ***Is It Magnetic or Nonmagnetic?***
AUTHOR: **Trudy Rising**
PUBLISHER: **Crabtree Publishing Company**
YEAR: **2012**
GENRE: **Non-Narrative Information**
SUMMARY: *From the What's the Matter? series, this book introduces magnetic and nonmagnetic as properties of matter that can be used to classify materials. It explains the "secret" to magnetic materials and explores the strength of different magnets as well as their uses.*

Time Needed

This lesson will take several class periods. Suggested scheduling is as follows:

Session 1: Engage with *That Magnetic Dog* Read-Aloud and **Explore** with Fishing with Magnets

Session 2: Explain with What Can You Catch with a Magnet? Poster, *Is It Magnetic or Nonmagnetic?* Read-Aloud, and Revisiting *That Magnetic Dog*

Session 3: Elaborate with Uses for Magnets

Session 4: Evaluate with Magnetic Solutions and The Day My Feet Were Magnets (Optional)

Materials

- Magnet warning signs page

For Fishing with Magnets (per team of 3 or 4 students):

- A container or tray with a large variety of both magnetic and nonmagnetic items to test for magnetic properties (see chart for suggestions)
- 1 30 cm piece of string
- 1 ceramic ring magnet or magnetic wand
- 1 pencil

Ceramic ring magnets and magnetic wands are available from

Educational Innovations Inc.
www.teachersource.com

Amazon
Amazon.com

Peel-and-stick adhesive business card magnets are available from

Amazon
Amazon.com

MAGNETIC ITEMS	NONMAGNETIC ITEMS
pipe cleaner	aluminum foil
steel paper clip	plastic paper clip
magnetite rock	small rock (other than magnetite)
stainless steel spoon	white plastic and silver-colored plastic spoons
steel bolt	toothpick or craft stick
steel washer	aluminum washer
steel wool	metallic-looking fabric or cotton ball
antique iron skeleton key	brass housekey
steel lid from a soda bottle	aluminum tab from a soda can
tumbled magnetic hematite stone	glass marble or tumbled glass pebble
magnetic foreign coins (such as UK copper-plated steel penny and 2 pence and UK nickel-plated steel 5 pence and 10 pence)	nonmagnetic coins (such as U.S. coins, including a penny—note that the vast majority of U.S. coins in circulation are nonmagnetic)

For What Can You Catch with a Magnet? (per team of 3 or 4 students)

- 1 piece of white card stock or poster paper, 9 x 12 or larger
- Crayons or markers
- Tape

For Revisiting That Magnetic Dog

- Assortment of keys
- Assortment of plastic and metal spoons
- Magnet

For Magnetic Solutions (per student)

- 1 magnet
  (*Note:* Additional materials will vary.)

For STEM Everywhere (per student)

- One 2 x 3 ½ in peel-and-stick adhesive business card magnet

Student Pages

- What Can You Catch with a Magnet?
- My Magnetic Solution
- STEM Everywhere

Background for Teachers

A *magnet* is an object or material that produces an invisible *magnetic field*. Within this field, a magnet attracts or repels other magnets and pulls on objects with iron in them. Magnetic force acts across distance—a magnet does not need to touch magnetic materials to act on them. A magnetic field is strongest around the *poles*, or ends, of a magnet. All magnets have a north pole and a south pole. If you hold two magnets so that their unlike (north and south) poles are close but not touching, you will feel the force of the magnets *attracting* each other. If you hold two magnets so that their like (north and north or south and south) poles are close but not touching, you will feel the force of the magnets *repelling* each other.

Although physicists consider "magnetic" materials to be those that can be magnetized, we are simplifying this classification for young learners. In the nonfiction book *Is It Magnetic or Nonmagnetic?*, any material that is attracted to a magnet is referred to as a *magnetic* material. Any material that is not attracted to a magnet is referred to as a *nonmagnetic* material. This lesson focuses on *magnetic* and *nonmagnetic* as properties of matter that can be used to sort, or classify, matter. A common misconception is that all metals are magnetic. In fact, only materials that contain iron, cobalt, or nickel are attracted to a magnet. We focus on the metals iron and steel (an iron *alloy*) as the most common magnetic materials because items made of cobalt and nickel are not nearly as familiar to students. After exploring these magnetic materials, students discover some uses for magnets and design a "magnetic" solution to a problem. In grades 3–5, students will learn more about magnetic force.

Students are engaged in several different science and engineering practices (SEPs) in this lesson. They use the SEP of asking questions and defining problems as they question why certain things are attracted to a magnet and others are not, and they define a simple classroom problem that can be solved using a magnet. Students are involved in planning and carrying out investigations as they test and sort materials by magnetic properties. The SEP of developing explanations and designing solutions is incorporated as students develop the explanation that not all metals are magnetic, and they design a solution to a problem using magnets and magnetic material. The crosscutting concept (CCC) of cause and effect is addressed as students learn that iron is the cause of some things sticking to a magnet.

> **WARNING**
>
> Magnets are used in a wide variety of electronic equipment. Placing a magnet close to such equipment may cause damage. Before using magnets in your classroom, make students aware that magnets should be kept away from electronic equipment. Also, keep magnets away from credit cards, videotapes, and any other materials that have information on a magnetic strip.

Learning Progressions

Below are the disciplinary core idea (DCI) grade band endpoints for grades K–2 and 3–5. These are provided to show how student understanding of the DCIs in this lesson will progress in future grade levels.

DCI	Grades K–2	Grades 3–5
PS1.A: Structure and Properties of Matter	• Matter can be described and classified by its observable properties.	• Measurements of a variety of properties can be used to identify materials.

Source: Willard, T., ed. 2015. *The NSTA quick-reference guide to the* NGSS: *Elementary school.* Arlington, VA: NSTA Press.

engage

That Magnetic Dog Read-Aloud

Connecting to the Common Core
Reading: Literature
INTEGRATION OF KNOWLEDGE AND IDEAS: 2.7

**Inferring**

Show the book *That Magnetic Dog* to the class. Introduce the author and illustrator. *Ask*

? What do you think this book might be about? (Answers will vary.)

Next, read the book aloud, then *ask*

? Why does the author describe the dog as "magnetic"? (She attracts people and food.)

? Have you ever heard of someone having a "magnetic personality"? What does that mean? (People are drawn or attracted to them.)

? What does magnetic mean? (Answers will vary.)

Making Connections:
Text to Self

Ask

? Have you ever explored with magnets? (Answers will vary.)

? What do you know about magnets? (Answers will vary.)

explore

Fishing with Magnets

Before you begin this phase of the lesson, copy the magnet warning signs on fluorescent paper and post them on computers and other electronic equipment in the classroom. Explain to students that magnets can damage electronic equipment like televisions and computers, so they must pay attention to the signs. Then *ask*

? What types of items do you think stick to a magnet? (Students may say that some or all metal items stick to a magnet.)

> **SEP: Analyzing and Interpreting Data**
> Compare predictions (based on prior experiences) to what occurred (observable events.

Split students into teams of three or four. Give each team a container or tray with a variety of magnetic and nonmagnetic items (see materials list for suggestions). Invite students to take a close look at the items, pick them up, and feel them. Then have them sort the items into three piles:

- Items they predict will stick to a magnet
- Items they predict will not stick to a magnet
- Items they are not sure will stick to a magnet

"FISHING" WITH A MAGNET

Have students discuss their thinking as they are sorting. When they have finished sorting, ask them to pick up one item that they predict will stick to the magnet and hold it up. *Ask*

? Why did you predict that item will stick? (Answers will vary, but students will typically put all of the metal items in this pile.)

Next, ask them to pick up one item they predict will not stick to the magnet, and *ask*

? Why did you predict that item won't stick? (Answers will vary.)

CCC: Patterns
Patterns in the natural and human designed world can be observed, used to describe phenomena, and used as evidence.

Then ask them to pick up one item of which they are unsure whether it will stick to a magnet, and *ask*

? What makes you unsure about that item? (Answers will vary.)

MAKING A POSTER

Finally, *ask*

? How can we find out which items will stick to a magnet? (Test them!)

Tell students that they are going to take turns "fishing" with a fishing pole made out of a magnet to see which items in the box they can "catch." Show students how to make the fishing pole by tying one end of a string around the end of a ceramic ring magnet or magnetic wand and the other end of the string to a pencil. Students are now ready to use their fishing poles to see what items their magnets will catch. Tell students to create two new piles as they take turns fishing:

1. Things that stick to the magnet
2. Things that do not stick to the magnet

explain

What Can You Catch with a Magnet? Poster

In teams, have students create a poster to present their findings to the rest of the class. They can do so by drawing a line down the center of a large piece of white card stock or poster paper and writing "Things That Stick" on the left side and "Things That Don't Stick" on the right side. Then have them tape the items that stick to the magnet onto the left side and the items that do not stick to the magnet onto the right side.

 *Writing*

Connecting to the Common Core
Writing
RESEARCH TO BUILD KNOWLEDGE: 2.8

After students are finished making their posters, pass out the What Can You Catch with a Magnet? student page and have them answer questions 1–3. (They will answer questions 1–4 after the read-

aloud.) Questions and possible responses are as follows:

1. What items can you "catch" with a magnet? (Answers will depend on the materials in each set.)

2. What do those items have in common? (Students may notice that many, but not all, of the metal items stick to the magnet.)

3. Why do you think those items stick to the magnet? (Students may infer that those items stick to the magnet because they are metal.)

Next, have them share their posters and explain their responses to questions 1–3 on the student page with the rest of the class. As they share, you can ask clarifying questions, such as:

? Why do you think so?

? What is your evidence?

? What surprised you?

At this point, many students may have proposed that the items that stick to the magnet are metal and the items that don't stick are not metal. Although this conclusion is not entirely correct, they are getting closer to the secret of magnetic materials.

You may want to demonstrate that a penny does not stick to a magnet, even though it is metal. Some metals stick to a magnet, but not all. Students may hypothesize that there is something "special" about the items that stick to the magnet.

Is It Magnetic or Nonmagnetic? Read-Aloud

Connecting to the Common Core
Reading: Informational Text
CRAFT AND STRUCTURE: 2.4, 2.5

Using Features of Nonfiction/ Chunking

Show students the cover of the book *Is It Magnetic or Nonmagnetic?*, and then show the table of contents and a few of the inside pages. *Ask*

? Is this a fiction or nonfiction book? (nonfiction)

? How can you tell? (Answers may include that it has a table of contents, photographs, bold-print words, and an index.)

Determining Importance

Explain that, because the book is nonfiction, you can enter the text at any point. You don't have to read the book from cover to cover if you are looking for specific information. Tell students that this book might be able to help them discover the secret of the materials that stick to a magnet. Ask students to signal (by giving a thumbs-up, touching their nose, or some other method) when they hear the answer to this question:

? What is "special" about the items that stick to a magnet?

Read the book aloud, stopping when the answer is revealed on page 7. Students should now understand that items stick to a magnet if they contain iron. That's the secret! *Ask*

? What do all of the items on the "Things That Stick" side of the poster have in common? (They all contain iron.)

? What do we call items that stick to a magnet? (magnetic)

> **SEP: Obtaining, Evaluating, and Communicating Information**
> Read grade-appropriate texts and/or use media to obtain scientific and/or technical information to determine patterns in and/or evidence about the natural and designed worlds.

Point out that many of the items that stick to a magnet are made of steel. Steel is a metal that contains iron. If they have a rock in their set of materials that sticks to the magnet, then the rock contains iron. If they have a spoon in their set that sticks to the magnet, then the spoon contains iron, and so on.

Then explain that objects that do not stick to a magnet are called nonmagnetic. These items do not contain iron. Students will notice that some of the metal items, such as aluminum, do not stick. That is because aluminum does not contain iron. The metal penny does not stick. That is because pennies do not contain iron. (Pennies are actually made of copper-coated zinc.)

Note: There are other metals, such as cobalt and nickel, that are magnetic, but iron is more common and more familiar to students.

Students can now use the scientific vocabulary to label their posters. They will label the side of the poster containing items that stick to a magnet with the word *magnetic* and the other side with the word *nonmagnetic*.

Determining Importance

Next, read the rest of the questions on the What Can You Catch with a Magnet? student page together, and ask students to listen for the answers as you continue reading the book through page 13.

Writing

> Connecting to the Common Core
> **Writing**
> RESEARCH TO BUILD KNOWLEDGE: 2.8

Stop reading after page 13 and have students answer questions 4–7. Questions and possible responses are as follows:

4. What do properties of matter describe? (Page 6: Properties of matter describe how something looks, feels, tastes, smells, or sounds. Properties can also tell us how something acts.)

5. Fill in the blanks: Materials that have a magnetic property can pull, or _____, objects with _____ in them. (Page 7: attract, iron)

6. What else have you learned about magnets from the book so far? (Answers will vary.)

7. What are you still wondering about magnets? (Answers will vary.)

Revisiting *That Magnetic Dog*

Monitoring Comprehension

Tell students that there was a sentence in *That Magnetic Dog* that didn't make sense to you. Reread the first page of the book, which states, "Magnets attract metal objects like keys and spoons." Then *ask*

? What does the word *attract* mean? (pull)

? Does that sentence make sense to you? Is it entirely correct to say, "Magnets attract metal objects, like keys and spoons"? (Based on what students have learned through the explore and explain phases of this lesson, they should be able to identify the sentence as being incorrect.)

? Why? What is your evidence? (Students should be able to share evidence from their testing that not all keys and spoons stick to a magnet. You may want to have students retest the keys and spoons in their sets with a magnet and share examples of exceptions to the statement that "Magnets attract metal objects, like keys and spoons.")

? Why don't all of the keys and spoons stick to a magnet? (Not all of the keys and spoons contain iron. There may be some old keys in their set that do contain iron, but most housekeys are now made of brass, which is an alloy, or mixture, of copper and zinc. Brass is often used for keys because it doesn't rust and is soft enough to easily be cut into the needed individual patterns.)

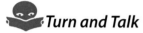**Turn and Talk**

Have students turn to a partner and discuss this question:

? How could we rewrite the sentence in the book to make it scientifically accurate, or correct?

(Possible answers include:

Magnets attract metal objects that contain iron.

Magnets attract some, but not all, metal objects.

Magnets attract keys and spoons that contain iron.)

Have pairs share their responses with the class.

elaborate

Uses for Magnets

Ask

? What are some uses for magnets? (Answers will vary.)

Show students the table of contents of *Is It Magnetic or Nonmagnetic? Ask*

? Which section do you think we should read to find out more about some of the uses for magnets? (Useful Magnets, page 14)

Read aloud pages 14–17 (you can skip the rest of the book or read it later if you wish), which share the different shapes and strengths of magnets as well as several different technologies that use magnets. For each of the technologies, *ask*

? What problem does the magnet solve?

Technology from the Book	Problem It Solves
Magnetic strip (page 14)	Holds and organizes cooking tools
Magnetic chess set (page 15)	Keeps the pieces from falling off the board
Magnetic can opener (page 15)	Holds the lid while the can is being opened
Scrapyard magnet (page 16)	Sorts the iron objects from the rest of the materials
Metal detector (page 17)	Finds metal objects underground

Next, *ask*

? Are there any useful magnets in our classroom? (Answers will vary.)

LOOKING FOR MAGNETS IN THE CLASSROOM

Give students time to walk around and discover any useful classroom magnets, then identify the problem that they solve. Some examples might include:

Classroom Magnet	Problem It Solves
Magnetic clip	Holds papers together on a whiteboard or other magnetic surface
Magnetic pouch	Holds and organizes objects
Magnetic cabinet latch	Keeps cabinet door closed
Refrigerator door magnet	Keeps refrigerator door sealed shut

Some students may know that motors and electronic devices like speakers, headphones, and computers also contain magnets.

evaluate

Magnetic Solutions

Tell students that they are going to have the chance to design a magnetic solution to a simple problem. *Ask*

? What does the word *solution* mean? (A solution is an answer to a problem.)

MAGNETIC SOLUTION

Explain that in this case, a solution is a device, toy, or game invented to solve a problem. *Ask*

? What "problem" does a toy or game solve? (A toy or game gives you something to do when you're bored, helps you have fun with your friends, entertains you, etc.)

Give each student a magnet (you can use the ring magnets from the explore phase or other magnets if you prefer). Students may choose to work together so that their solutions employ the use of multiple magnets.

Brainstorm some solutions together, such as:

- a magnetic pouch made of an envelope and a magnet that holds pencils or supplies in a student's locker or on the side of their desk
- a paper holder that holds a small stack of paper together between two magnets
- a magnetic metal detector made of a magnet attached to a pencil or a stick that can that pull out magnetic materials buried in sand or rice
- a magnetic picture frame that attaches a picture to a locker door
- a magnet-powered toy car that moves across a desk
- a magnetic metal collector that pulls paper clips out of a glass of water
- a magnetic toy sorter made of a magnet on a string that separates metal toy cars from other toys
- a magnetic paper clip maze made of a thin paper plate or aluminum pie pan with a maze drawn on it

Once you brainstorm a few solutions, students will get the idea!

After they have designed their solution (or toy or game), have them test and evaluate it, then redesign it if necessary. Next, pass out the My Magnetic Solution student page and have them draw and name their solution, describe how it works, identify which materials in their solution are magnetic and which materials are nonmagnetic, and explain why they chose those materials.

Connecting to the Common Core
Writing
TEXT AND PURPOSES: 2.3

Optional Writing Extension: The Day My Feet Were Magnets

Ask students to think about what would happen if they woke up one morning to find that their feet had mysteriously been turned into very strong magnets. Brainstorm ideas together by asking questions such as:

? When you woke up, how would you know that your feet were magnets?

? What would your feet look like or be made of?

? How would they feel?

? What things would be attracted to your feet? Why?

? What problems would you have if your feet were very strong magnets?

? What advantages or superpowers would you have if your feet were very strong magnets?

? How would your day be different if your feet were very strong magnets?

Then have them write a story on their own, or you may choose to write a class story.

MATERIALS FOR DESIGN A GAME ACTIVITY

STEM Everywhere

Give students the STEM Everywhere student page as a way to involve their families and extend their learning. They can do the activity with an adult helper and share their results with the class.

Opportunities for Differentiated Instruction

This box lists questions and challenges related to the lesson that students may select to research, investigate, or innovate. Students may also use the questions as examples to help them generate their own questions. These questions can help you move your students from the teacher-directed investigation to engaging in the science and engineering practices in a more student-directed format.

Extra Support

For students who are struggling to meet the lesson objectives, provide a question and guide them in the process of collecting research or help them design procedures or solutions.

Extensions

For students with high interest or who have already met the lesson objectives, have them choose a question (or pose their own question), conduct their own research, and design their own procedures or solutions.

After selecting one of the questions in the box or formulating their own question, students can individually or collaboratively make predictions, design investigations or surveys to test their predictions, collect evidence, devise explanations, design solutions, or examine related resources. They can communicate their findings through a science notebook, at a poster session or gallery walk, or by producing a media project.

Research

Have students brainstorm researchable questions:

? How are magnets made?

? What are magnetic poles?

? How is Earth like a magnet?

Investigate

Have students brainstorm testable questions to be solved through science or math:

? Can magnetic force pass through water?

? Can magnetic force pass through wood, plastic, or other materials?

? Are larger magnets stronger than smaller magnets?

Innovate

Have students brainstorm problems to be solved through engineering:

? Can you design a maze that uses magnets and magnetic items?

? Can you design a magic trick that uses magnets and magnetic items?

? Can you make a magnet?

More Books to Read

Branley, F. M. 2016. *What makes a magnet?* New York: HarperCollins.
Summary: This updated version of the Let's-Read-and-Find-Out Science book explains the basic principles of magnetism.

Enz, T. 2020. *Discover magnets*. North Mankato, MN: Pebble Books.
Summary: Clear text and colorful photographs describe magnets, how they work, and where they are used.

Rosinsky, N. 2003. *Magnets: Pulling together, pushing apart*. Minneapolis: Picture Window Books.
Summary: Simple text and illustrations, accompanied by fun facts, explain how magnets work, why Earth is really a giant magnet, how a compass works, and more. Includes simple experiments, table of contents and glossary, and a website with links to other safe, fun websites related to the book's content.

Weakland, M. 2011. *Magnets push, magnets pull*. Mankato, MN: Capstone Press.
Summary: This book explains the basics of magnetism with simple text and photographs.

NO MAGNET ZONE

KEEP MAGNETS AWAY

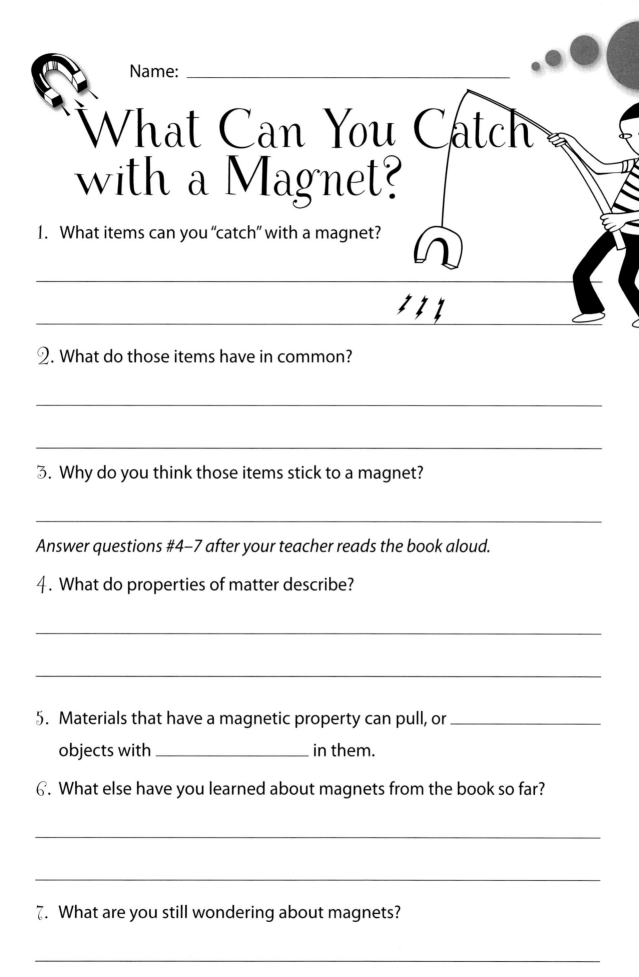

What Can You Catch with a Magnet?

1. What items can you "catch" with a magnet?

_____

_____

2. What do those items have in common?

_____

_____

3. Why do you think those items stick to a magnet?

_____

Answer questions #4–7 after your teacher reads the book aloud.

4. What do properties of matter describe?

_____

_____

5. Materials that have a magnetic property can pull, or _____

objects with _____ in them.

6. What else have you learned about magnets from the book so far?

_____

_____

7. What are you still wondering about magnets?

_____

Name: _____

My Magnetic Solution

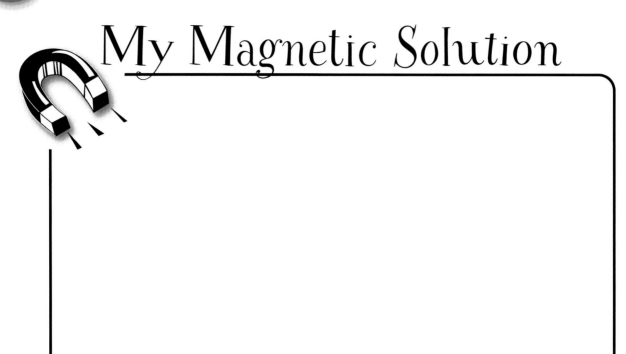

Name of solution: _____

How does it work? _____

_____

What parts are magnetic? _____

_____

Why did you use magnetic materials for those parts? _____

_____

What parts are nonmagnetic? _____

_____

Why did you use nonmagnetic materials for those parts?

_____

_____

National Science Teaching Association

Name: _____

STEM Everywhere

Dear Families,

At school, we have been learning about how **some materials are magnetic and other are nonmagnetic**. To find out more, ask your learner questions such as:

- What did you learn?
- What was your favorite part of the lesson?
- What are you still wondering?

At home, you can make your own refrigerator magnet, then use it to find magnetic materials around the house. Caution: Do not use magnets on electronic devices!

First, choose a template to color (or use the blank one and design your own). Then cut it out and attach it to a peel-and-stick adhesive business card magnet.

Use your magnet to test materials around the house. What materials are magnetic?

_____

_____

_____

_____

_____

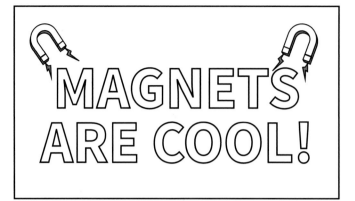

MAGNETS ARE COOL!

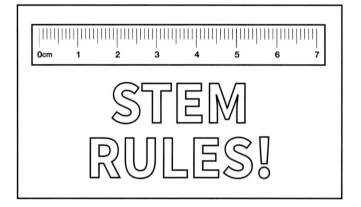

STEM RULES!

SCIENCE ROCKS!

National Science Teaching Association